Write It Right
with
Step by Step
by
Edna Mae Burnam

To my grandson, David Bender

ISBN 978-1-4234-3604-1

WILLIS MUSIC

EXCLUSIVELY DISTRIBUTED BY

HAL•LEONARD®
CORPORATION
7777 W. BLUEMOUND RD. P.O. BOX 13819 MILWAUKEE, WI 53213

© 1980 by The Willis Music Co.
International Copyright Secured   All Rights Reserved

For all works contained herein:
Unauthorized copying, arranging, adapting, recording or public performance is an infringement of copyright.
Infringers are liable under the law.

Visit Hal Leonard Online at
www.halleonard.com

TO THE TEACHER

The written work in this book is designed to correlate exactly with Edna Mae Burnam's STEP BY STEP—Book Six.

At the beginning of each lesson, at the top of the page, is a notation giving the exact page in the correlated STEP BY STEP book at which the respective WRITE IT RIGHT lessons may be introduced. (Each lesson is planned on the musical steps which have been introduced up to and including this page.)

The WRITE IT RIGHT lessons will both train the student to be accurate and afford the teacher a means of checking the student's comprehension of the musical steps which he or she is learning.

A special effort has been made to incorporate variety in the written work and to choose subject matter which is appealing to the student.

I sincerely hope that the WRITE IT RIGHT lessons will be an enjoyable experience.

Edna Mae Burnam

When the student reaches page 9 of Edna Mae Burnam's STEP BY STEP — Book Six, he is ready to do Lesson One.

LESSON ONE

STEREO SYSTEM

This stereo is playing a record. There are eight different pieces
on this record, and each piece is in a different key.
Write the right name of each key in the boxes.

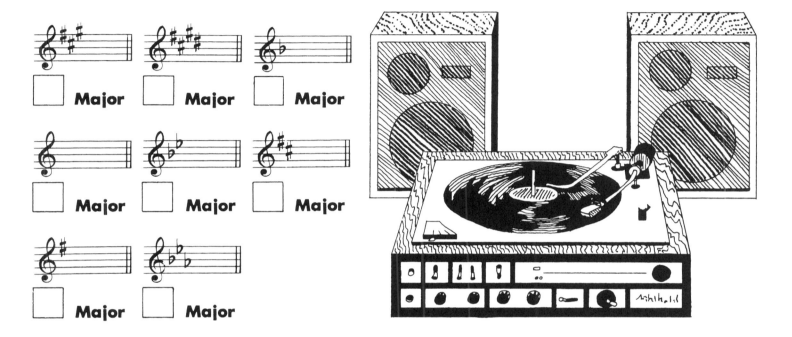

HELICOPTER

This helicopter takes off.
Write the right finger markings
for the **staccato** repeated notes.
If you get all of them right, you may
have a ride in the helicopter.

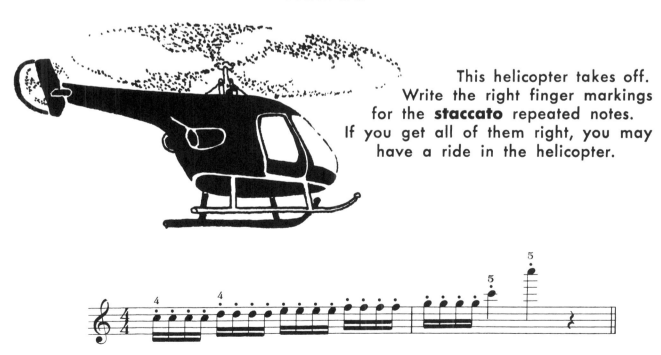

© MCMLXXX by The Willis Music Co.
International Copyright Secured
Printed in U.S.A.

4

SPRAY PERFUME

Here is a bottle of spray perfume.
When it is used, how long will the fragrance last?
Find the answer by adding up the counts
contained in the line of notes.

Write the right answer in the box.

BAR LINES

Draw bar lines in the right places for this line of notes.

QUESTIONS

What does **giocoso** mean?

_____

Is it good to change fingers on
staccato repeated notes?

_____

Is a dotted eighth note often
followed by a sixteenth note —
like this?

_____

LESSON TWO

A FOUNTAIN

Write the right
letter names of
the notes in
the boxes.

APPLES

How many seeds are there in each apple?

Find the right answer by adding up the counts contained in
each line of notes located below the apples.

Write the totals in the boxes.

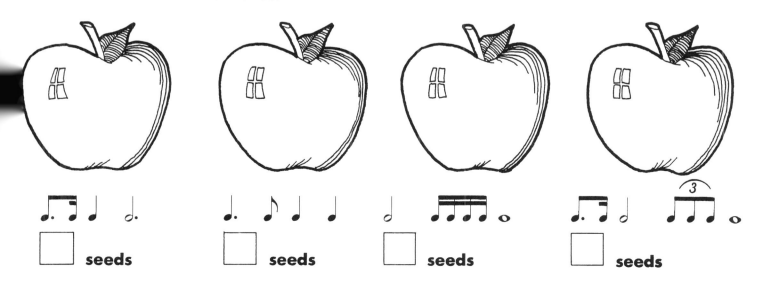

☐ **seeds** ☐ **seeds** ☐ **seeds** ☐ **seeds**

6

LADDER

Write the right name of each key signature.

If you get all of them right, you will climb the ladder without stumbling.

Major

Major

Major

Major

Major

Major

Major

Major

Major

BEACH BALL

This beach ball is decorated with different kinds of notes.

Draw a circle around each grace note.

QUESTIONS

Does **grace note** receive a count? _____

Is a **grace note** always higher than the note into which it snips? _____

Does **lesto** mean quick and lively? _____

Does **giocoso** mean merrily? _____

Does **pedal simile** mean easy pedaling? _____

When the student reaches page 23 of Edna Mae Burnam's STEP BY STEP — Book Six, he is ready to do Lesson Three.

LESSON THREE

A SINGING FENCE

This fence is singing half steps. Most of the half steps are either
from a white key to a black key, or from a black key to a white key;
but there are a few places where the half step is from a **white** key to
a **white** key. Put a circle around those places.

DRUM ROLL

Write a **grace notes drum roll**
for each of the accented notes.

WOODPECKER

This woodpecker made a hole in the tree so that he could store acorns.
How many acorns has he already stored away?
You can find the answer by adding up the
counts contained in the line of notes.

Put the answer in the box.

CHROMATIC SCALE

Write the right fingering for this **chromatic scale.**

QUESTIONS

What is the distance between any key
and the next key up or down?

What fingers are used in playing
a chromatic scale?

Does a chromatic scale always
begin on **C**?

When the student reaches page 28 of Edna Mae Burnam's STEP BY STEP — Book Six, he is ready to do Lesson Four.

9

LESSON FOUR

HUMMING BIRDS

Draw a line from
each humming bird
to the right flower
it will fly to
for pollen.

FIND THE ERROR

Here are two columns of notes.
The notes in column one match — in time value — the notes in column two.
In one row — they do not match!
Put a large **X** before the row that is not right.

Column One		Column Two

CAR KEY

Here are several car keys. Find the right key for this car.

Draw a line from the key to the car.

BAR LINES

Draw bar lines in the right places for each line of notes.

QUESTIONS

Is **E sharp** a black key sharp?　　　　　_____

Is **C sharp** a white key sharp?　　　　　_____

Is **D sharp** a black key sharp?　　　　　_____

Is **B flat** a black key flat?　　　　　_____

Is **F flat** a white key flat?　　　　　_____

How many sharps are there in
the key of **F sharp major**?　　　　　_____

LESSON FIVE

FIRE PLACE

A big log is burning in this fire place.
How many hours will it be before the big log burns up?
Find the answer by adding up the counts contained in the line of notes.
Write the right answer in the box.

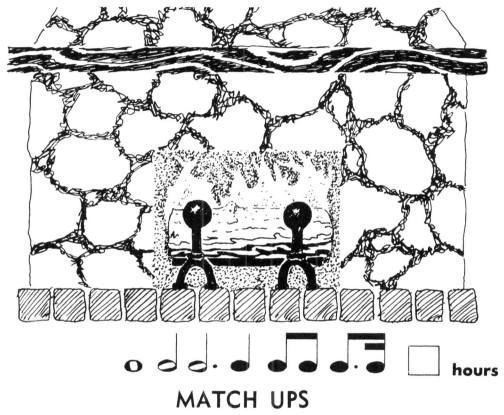

☐ **hours**

MATCH UPS

Draw a line from each meaning in
column one to the match up in
column two.

one

octave higher

octave lower

rolled chord

a half step

a grace note

pedal mark

chromatic passage

two

A SPOTTED SNAKE

Write the right
names of the
spot notes.
If you get all
of them right,
the snake will
not be poisonous.

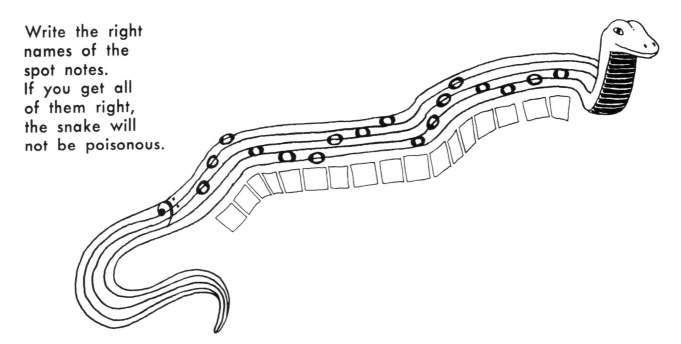

MUSIC MAY HAVE

M _ L O _ Y   _ N _   H _ R M O N Y

QUESTIONS

When you see the sign for a rolled chord,
do you begin the roll from the top note?   _____

Is music sometimes — for convenience sake —
printed on three staves?   _____

What are the names of the six sharps
in the key of **F sharp major**?   _____

When the student reaches page 39 of Edna Mae Burnam's STEP BY STEP — Book Six, he is ready to do Lesson Six.

13

LESSON SIX

UMBRELLA

When it rains, this umbrella hears a lovely rain song.

Write the right names of the notes and the song will be clear.

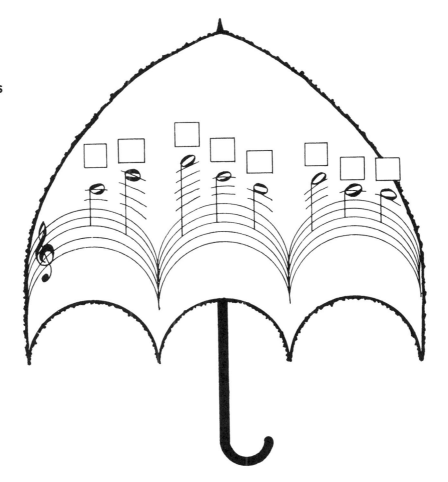

MAIL BOX

How many letters are there in this mail box?

To find the answer, add up the counts contained. in this line of notes and rests.

Write the right answer in the box.

PORTABLE RADIOS

Each radio is playing in a different key.
Write the right key for each one.

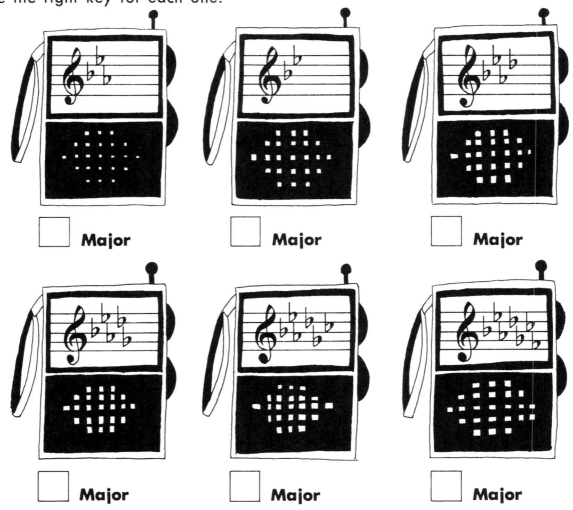

☐ **Major**   ☐ **Major**   ☐ **Major**

☐ **Major**   ☐ **Major**   ☐ **Major**

BAR LINES

Draw bar line in the right places for this line of notes.

QUESTIONS

When you see this sign ¢
does it mean to play **waltz time**?   _____

Is this sign called **alla breve**?   _____

Does **alla breve** mean that the piece
should be played twice as fast?   _____

When the student reaches page 44 of Edna Mae Burnam's STEP BY STEP — Book Six, he is ready to do Lesson Seven.

15

LESSON SEVEN

WINDOW SHADES

These window shades are being raised. (Remember, when a sharp sign
is placed before a note, it means to play the next key up.)
Draw a line from each window to the right key on the keyboard.

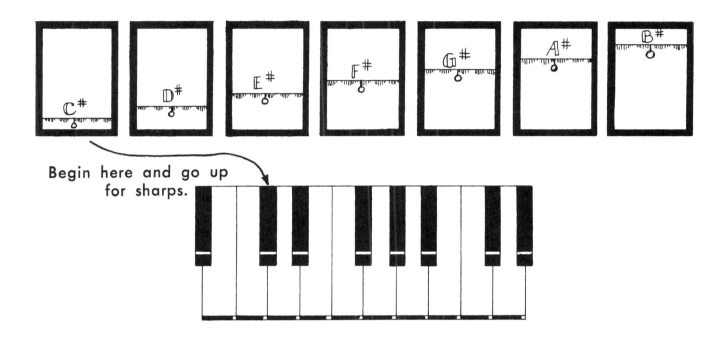

These window shades are being lowered. (Remember, when a flat sign
is placed before a note, it means the next key down.)
Draw a line from each window to the right key on the keyboard.

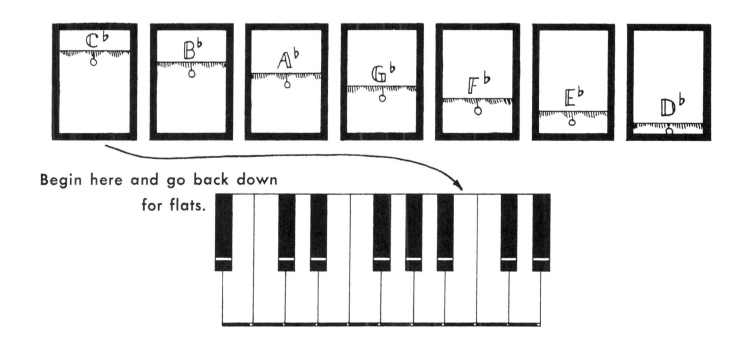

SKATE BOARD

Skate up a hill.

Is this a scale?_____

Is this a chromatic scale?_____

KEY SIGNATURE

G major has ☐ sharps.   **B major** has ☐ sharps.

D major has ☐ sharps.   **F# major** has ☐ sharps.

A major has ☐ sharps.   **C# major** has ☐ sharps.

E major has ☐ sharps.

A DOOR

The door is locked.

Draw a line from the door to the key which will unlock it.

C♭ Major

G♭ Major

QUESTIONS

Does **simile** mean in the same manner?   _____

Does **lesto** mean lively and quick?   _____

LESSON EIGHT

CHURCH BELLS

These bells ring when it is time for church to begin.
In order to find out at what time service begins in each church,
add up the counts contained in the groups of notes located below
each bell.
Write the right answers in the boxes.

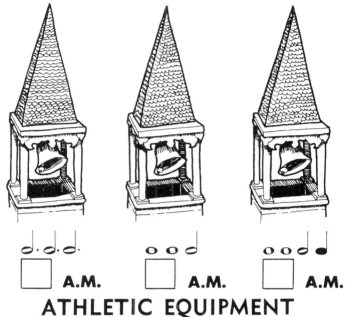

ATHLETIC EQUIPMENT

Decorate each item of athletic equipment with the signs indicated.

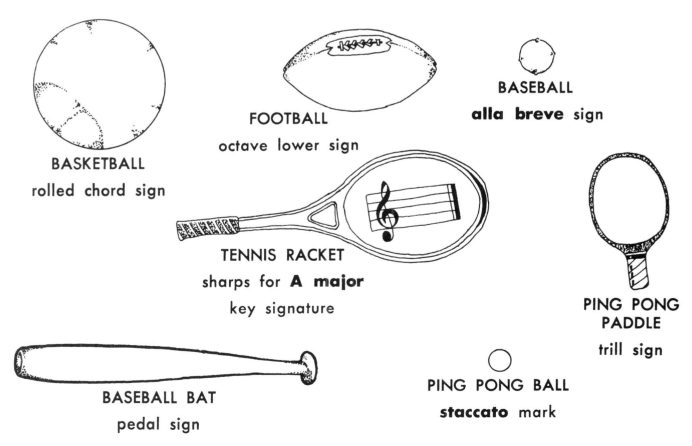

BASKETBALL
rolled chord sign

FOOTBALL
octave lower sign

BASEBALL
alla breve sign

TENNIS RACKET
sharps for **A major**
key signature

**PING PONG
PADDLE**
trill sign

BASEBALL BAT
pedal sign

PING PONG BALL
staccato mark

SENTENCES

allegretto

The program on TV was [   ] .

dolce

The organ music was played [   ] .

ritard.

The music box played [   ] until it stopped.

CROSS OVERS

Draw circles around all of the notes and chords played by the left hand.

QUESTIONS

Is this a trill sign? *tr*〰〰〰〰 _____

Are the notes of a rolled chord
held down as they are struck,
until the whole chord is played? _____

How many flats are there in the
key of **C flat Major**? _____

What are the names of these flats? _____

19

When the student reaches page 53 of Edna Mae Burnam's STEP BY STEP — Book Six, he is ready to do Lesson Nine.

LESSON NINE

WHEEL BARROW

How many buckets of rocks will this wheel barrow carry?

To find the answer, add up the counts contained in the row of notes.

Write the total in the box.

SENTENCES

The pin wheel will ⟦ ⟧ around when a breeze blows.

The canary sings a ⟦ ⟧ in his song.

The rowboat goes ⟦ **rit.** ⟧ as it goes to shore.

A water skier takes off ⟦ **Presto** ⟧.

COPY CAT

Here are two measures of notes.

Write the same letter name notes above the staff, using leger lines.

Begin here. →

TYPEWRITER

How many words a minute does the typist type when she uses this typewriter?

Find the answer by adding up the counts contained in the line of notes and rests.

Write the right answer in the box.

QUESTIONS

Does this sign *tr*〰〰〰 mean to keep repeating the same note **staccato**?   _____

Does this sign ∞ mean to hold this note longer?   _____

Does this sign C mean **4/4** meter?   _____

Does this sign ₵ mean **alla breve**?   _____

Is this smaller ♪ note called a **grace note**?   _____

Does a **grace note** receive one count?   _____

Lesson Ten is a review correlated with all of Edna Mae Burnam's STEP BY STEP — Book Six.

LESSON TEN

REVIEW

FINAL - NOTES

Write the right letter names of the notes in the boxes.

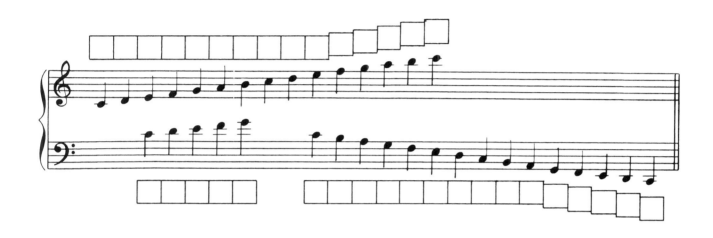

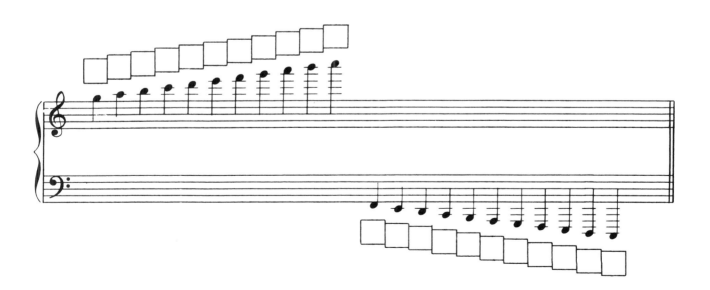

FINALE – KEY SIGNATURES

Write the right name of each key signature and write the right
letter names of the sharps or flats in each key — in the correct order.

no sharps or flats ☐ major

one sharp _____ ☐ major

two sharps _____ ☐ major

three sharps _____ ☐ major

four sharps _____ ☐ major

five sharps _____ ☐ major

six sharps _____ ☐ major

seven sharps _____ ☐ major

one flat _____ ☐ major

two flats _____ ☐ major

three flats _____ ☐ major

four flats _____ ☐ major

five flats _____ ☐ major

six flats _____ ☐ major

seven flats _____ ☐ major

WHIZ QUIZ - WORDS

Draw a line from each word (or pair of words) in column one
to the right meaning in column two.

one	two
giocoso	merrily
lesto	lively and quick
crescendo	gradually softer
diminuendo	gradually louder
dolce	in the same manner
simile	soft and sweetly
half step	shortest distance between two keys
chromatic passage	series of consecutive half steps moving up or down

22

WHIZ QUIZ
SIGNS

Draw a line from each word or group of words in column one to the matching sign in column two.

one	two
alla breve	
grace note	
rolled chord	$\frac{6}{8}$
six counts to a measure	¢
a turn	tr ～～～
trill	∞
octave higher	8 - - - - ⌐
octave lower	8 - - - - ⌐
pedal	

BAR LINES

Draw bar lines in the right places for this line of notes.

QUESTIONS

In $\frac{4}{4}$ meter, what kind of note receives one count? _____

In $\frac{6}{8}$ meter, what kind of note receives one count? _____

Is this a half step up? _____

Is this a half step down? _____

Is **B sharp** a white key sharp? _____

Is **F flat** a white key flat? _____

Will you always love music? _____

Certificate of Merit

This is to certify that

_____

has successfully completed

EDNA MAE BURNAM'S
WRITE IT RIGHT

_____Teacher

Date _____